The Orchard

Published by A & C Black (Publishers) Limited
35 Bedford Row, London WC1R 4JH

© Vanessa Luff 1991

A CIP catalogue record for this book is available from the British Library

ISBN 0-7136-3213-5

Apart from any fair dealing for the purposes of research or private study, or criticism or review, as permitted under the Copyright, Designs and Patents Act, 1988, this publication may be reproduced, stored or transmitted, in any form or by any means, only with the prior permission in writing of the publishers, or in the case of reprographic reproduction in accordance with the terms of licences issued by the Copyright Licensing Agency. Inquiries concerning reproduction outside those terms should be sent to the publishers at the above named address.

Typeset by Spectrum Typesetting Ltd, London
Printed in Hong Kong by Wing King Tong Ltd

The Orchard

Vanessa Luff

A & C Black · London

During the mild spring weather, small buds begin to swell on the twigs of the apple tree.

Birds collect grass, twigs and moss for their nests, which they build among the tree's leafy branches.

Bullfinches and other birds like to peck off the buds, which are bursting into flower.

Bees visit the apple blossom to collect nectar. They take pollen from one flower to another and help tiny apples to form.

The blossom drops from the apple tree and tiny apples begin to grow in its place. These hard green apples won't be ready to eat until the autumn.

Over long summer days, the apples ripen.
As they grow, they become sweeter.

The branches of the apple tree are heavy with ripening fruit. Under the tree, hens watch over their new chicks and look for insects and seeds to eat.

Summer showers bring on a final spurt of growth and the apples are ready to be picked. They are kept in a store away from the frost.

Some of the apples fall to the ground. These windfall apples rot or are eaten by animals. But their pips may sink into the soil and grow into new apple trees.

Dead leaves swirl around the orchard. A hedgehog gets ready to hibernate and geese arrive from the North.

The orchard is tidied up for its winter rest. The trees are pruned and cut branches are burnt on a big bonfire.

The orchard looks bleak and bare. The last apples from the store are thrown to the birds.

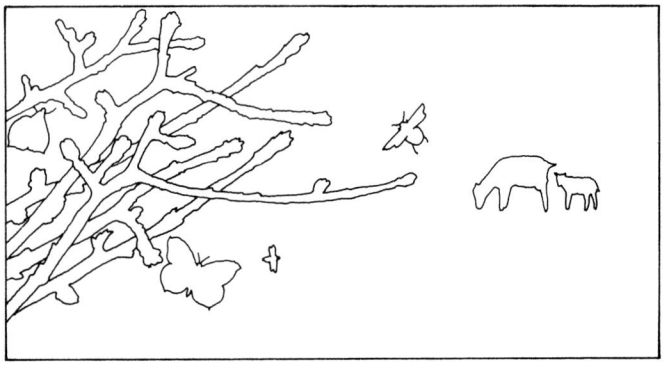

During the cold winter months, the orchard rests. But spring is a time of vigorous growth, especially for the apple tree: tight buds burst from their protective scales to reveal bright green leaves.

After the long cold winter, bees and brimstone butterflies eagerly look for nectar.

Goats are let out of their winter shelter to graze on the new sweet grass.

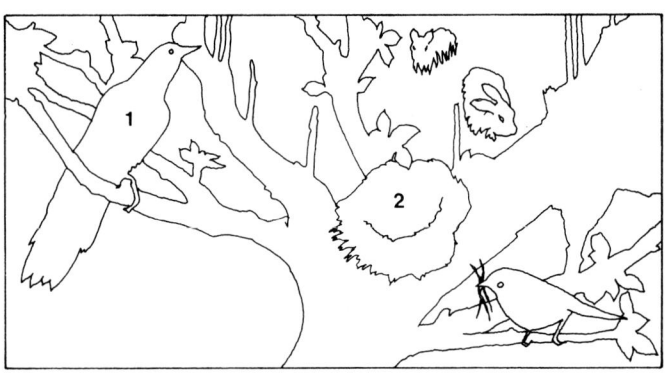

Light and water help the tree to grow. Each bud unfolds into a rosette of leaves, which are bright green with velvety undersides. Soon after the leaves open, the flower buds will begin to show.

The tree provides homes and a source of food for animals and insects. Birds build their nests in the leafy part of the tree, where it is safe and sheltered. The cuckoo (1) needs to find a nest in which to leave her eggs. She eyes the robin's nest (2), but it proves unsuitable.

Rabbits nibble the high grass. Daffodils are in flower.

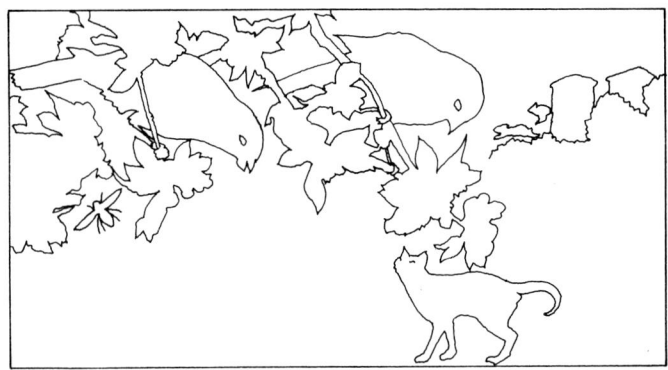

The apple leaves grow and darken in colour. Flower buds on the twigs turn deep pink. Birds can ruin the apple crop by nipping off the buds before they have a chance to grow. Many farmers place nets over the trees or put tin foil on the branches to scare the birds away.

Before the buds flower, bee hives are moved into the orchard. The flowers' smell, colour and shape attract bees looking for nectar and pollen, which they store in combs in the hive. At the end of the summer, the bee-keeper will remove the combs, slice away the wax coverings and take out the honey.

The buds open into pale pink and white flowers. On a warm day, the blossom hums with bees.

Bees move from flower to flower in search of nectar. Pollen from the stamens (the male part of the flower) sticks to the bee's hairy body. When the bee visits another flower, the pollen brushes off on to the stigma (the female part of the flower). The bees pollinate the blossom and this pollination enables tiny apples to form.

The crab spider is perfectly camouflaged. It grabs a bee, which is searching for nectar.

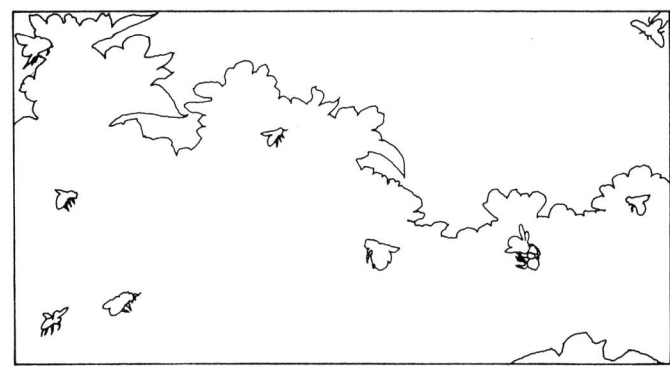

Some of the apple trees grow up against the orchard wall. Small green apples show underneath the petals of pollinated flowers.

Swallows spend the winter in the southern hemisphere and return to build nests, lay eggs and hatch their young.

The cuckoo found a place to leave her egg. She took an egg from the hedge sparrow's nest and replaced it with her own. Now the hedge sparrow has to work very hard collecting insects to feed the huge cuckoo fledgling, which she is fostering.

Squirrels are expert climbers. They live in treetop drays, which are dome-shaped nests made from twigs and moss.

The apples are growing in the sunshine, but they are still hard and they taste sour. On the bottom of each apple, the dried up parts of the flower shrivel gradually and fall away.

Butterflies skim over the lush grass, which is dotted with wild flowers; these might include clover, dandelions, meadow buttercups and ox-eye daisies.

House martins feast on swarms of midges and other small insects in the air.

Looper caterpillars (1) munch the apple leaves, but many are caught by wasps (2), taken to the wasps' nest, and fed to grubs.

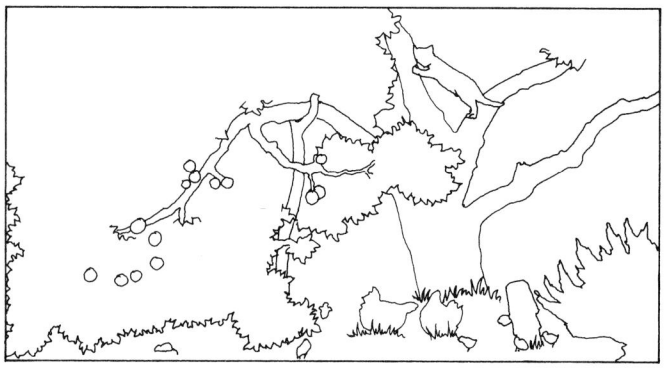

Summer passes; the apples swell and turn russet red. The weight of a good crop pulls down the tree's branches, which have to be propped up to stop them breaking.

Hens watch over their broods of chicks. Under the apple tree, there is plenty of food for them. They scratch around the earth and pick up the apple sawfly and the codling moth grub, pests likely to cause infestations of maggoty apples in next year's crop.

The grass is left uncut, giving wild flowers such as rosebay willow herb, yarrow and hawkbit a chance to flourish.

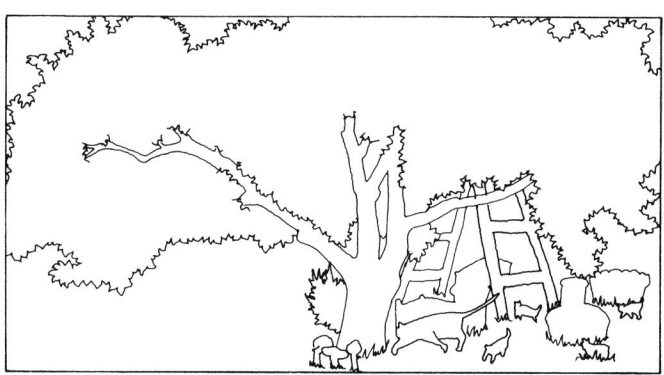

The days are becoming shorter and it is time to harvest the crop; the apples taste sweet, their pips are brown and the join between stalk and twig is easily broken. Some of the apples are stored for the winter months.

Various fungi grow up through the damp soil. Some fungi are poisonous.

Windfall fruit falls to the ground and bruises. These apples have been left to rot, but various animals such as the wood mouse (1), large red slug (2), wasp (3) and Roman snail (4) feed off the apples' sweet flesh as they decompose.

When the fruit rots, the pips drop to the ground. Then pigs wander in the orchard, eating the last of the apples. They fertilize the soil with their droppings. Some of the apple pips may germinate and grow into new apple trees.

Autumn arrives swiftly and the orchard prepares for winter. Nourishment from the leaves is drawn back into the trees. The leaves lose chlorophyll, turn yellow and a strong wind or sharp frost can make them drop within a few days. The leaves rot, turn into humus and become part of the topsoil.

A hedgehog fattens itself up for hibernation. Rooks stalk across the grass, hoping to find worms and grubs exposed by the raked up leaves.

Geese fly in 'V' formations across the sky. They have migrated from the cold northern lands to spend the winter on nearby fields and marshes.

In the winter months, food for birds is scarce. At dusk, an owl hunts down its prey. A robin eats the white berries of the evergreen mistletoe, a parasitic plant, which draws nourishment from a host apple tree.

The trees are pruned; whip-like shoots are trimmed and old or diseased branches cut out. This encourages fruiting buds to grow, keeps the tree in a manageable condition and prevents disease. The cuttings are burnt and give off the distinctive smell of apple smoke.

Hungry starlings feed on the last apples from the winter store, which have been thrown into the snow. In the afternoon, the starlings fly off to roost in huge flocks with thousands of other starlings. They will spend the night together in woods or on buildings in the middle of towns.

Now, the apple trees look stark and lifeless, but they are just resting and conserving energy. Buds, which were formed during the summer, will develop when the warm weather comes and over the long summer days ahead.